River to River, Year After Year

RAGBRAI Through the Lens of Register Photographers

presented by

RAGBRAI

The Des Moines Register
Full of **Life**
DesMoines**Register**.com

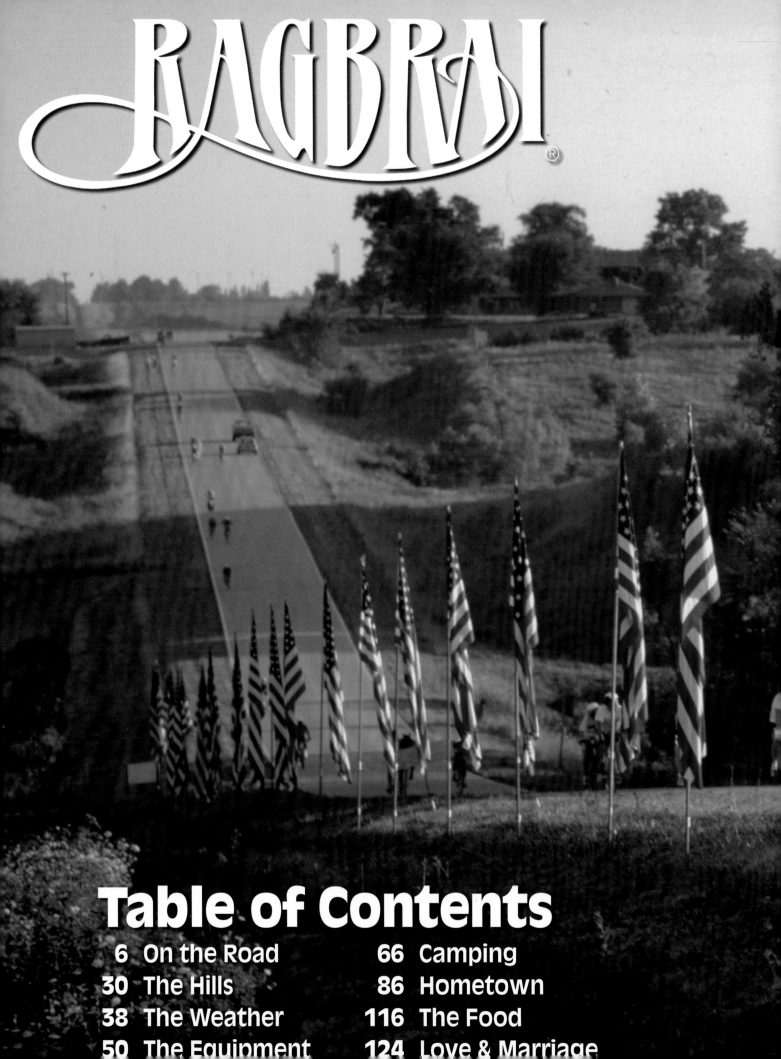

RAGBRAI

Table of Contents

RAGBRAI riders receive a patriotic welcome from Brooklyn residents, 1991.

SOMETIMES GOOD PICTURES just fall into your camera. For Des Moines Register photographers, events like the Iowa State Fair, sports tournaments, big spot news events and dramatic changes in weather usually produce the most dramatic and story telling images. And usually the pictures almost beg shooters to make them.

But no yearly event we cover is as easy to photograph as RAGBRAI, the Register's Annual Great Bicycle Ride Across Iowa. Pictures -good pictures- almost sneak into our cameras. They happen before the ride, after it ends and almost every moment in-between.

How 10,000 riders can be so joyful after sitting on little more than a thinly padded 2x4 for several hours, not to mention peddling during sometimes frightful weather conditions, baffles we who bear witness. But the key is in the mode of transportation. The bicycle is a very personal modus transporti. It can be ridden alone or with a large team and stopped in a short space if necessary.

It's at those stops that RAGBRAI comes into its own. Whether it's an overnight stop in a city, a pie-laden lunch stop in a town or just a pause at a farmhouse offering a cold drink from their well, that's where riders meet Iowans. It's the joining of those two elements that cements RAGBRAI. That's where the spirit of Iowa is revealed.

Those meetings make the best RAGBRAI pictures. Usually they are accidental, two strangers taking up conversation on the main street of a town. The resident could be (and often is) a retired farmer wearing blue-striped overalls. The rider, coated in multi-colored Spandex could be a college president or an advertising executive or the Secretary of the Air Force, or just an average person you see on the street. The connections made there during RAGBRAI week are memorable and go far toward the common human understanding that sometimes seems so short in other parts of the world. We hope the pictures here will help you enjoy that connection.

A little history on photo coverage of RAGBRAI

Although RAGBRAI has always presented surprises to the photographers who cover the ride, no surprise was greater than 1973 when the photo department was told about the ride and the assignment to cover this trek across the state. That initial Great Six-Day Bicycle Ride across Iowa and the years of RAGBRAI that followed have held unique memories for the riders, the towns and those of us who've brought the ride to our readers.

In 1975, Register Executive Editor Mike Gartner discovered I was planning to ride and asked me if I'd shoot some pictures while on my "vacation." I said sure, in exchange for meals and a motel room each night, and a deal was struck.

With two of my brothers, a handlebar pack for one camera and film and a seat pack for an extra lens, I covered RAGBRAI III from the leather seat of my Raleigh Grand Prix. Shooting from a bicycle proved a splendid platform, giving me access to places along the route that a car would find hazardous.

Typically I'd shoot from breakfast to lunch. Our summer intern, Jim Wong, fixed the problem of getting the pictures back to The Register. He'd throttle up his little Honda motorcycle each day and meet me at a prearranged place, usually a courthouse or local police station. With my film and identifying notes, he'd ride back to Des Moines where photo lab technicians Jack Brinton or Paul Caster would process and print the pictures.

It was on that 1975 ride that I became convinced of the goodness of RAGBRAI. My brothers Gordon and Paul left Boone on the morning of Day Four without breakfast, foolishly thinking we'd find plenty to eat along the way.

This assumption was foolish for two reasons. First, RAGBRAI was only three years old and had yet to reach to the sprawling, mul serviced event it is today. Second, and even more foolishly, because my younger brother Paul is diabetic, going without food for his bo to process was begging for trouble.

Without so much as a mulberry tree along the route we rolled into tiny Luther (population under 500) searching for food, any food. Two blocks off the route we spied a house with lots of bikes in front. It was a café and it was jam-packed with riders, all hungry We walked straight in, past the full tables and the riders who were helping wait tables and into the kitchen.

The overwhelmed owner, Louise Shreve, hardly looked at me when I demanded, "I need a plate of food for my little brother." Sh just handed me one loaded with eggs, bacon and toast. Nothing she could have done would have been more welcome. I'll always remember her simple act of unselfish, life-saving kindness.

Later Shreve (see page 118) told me why she was under-prepared. "They told me not many people would stop." The Taylor brothers and several other riders stayed through lunch to help her with dishes and clean up.

Much like my film camera days on the route, RAGBRAI had simple beginnings. But the photographers of The Des Moines Register soon began upgrading their time, equipment and technology spent on the increasingly popular event. As RAGBRAI numbers reached into the thousands, Register photographers starte covering the event in groups. As simple Schwinn bikes with riders cut-offs were replaced by titanium road racers and spandex, simple black-and-white film operations were replaced by large processing tanks in hotel rooms and fast color film.

Today the film is gone. Register photographers shoot with digital cameras, transmitting their photos back to the newsroom vi cellular phones hooked-up to laptop computers. What used to take the better part of an afternoon, getting pictures back to the paper, now takes minutes.

Even though RAGBRAI has swelled in participants and the growing legions of support personnel and vehicles, it has retained that one camera charm I found 27 years ago. As you flip through the pages of this visual record, you'll find the main things that are different from year to year are the hairstyles, clothes or the occasion bicycle upgrade. The smiles along the miles are the same now as back then. We've left the captions on the photos pretty much as the would have appeared at the time they were published in the paper make you feel as though you're traveling with us through each year ride. Enjoy your trip through the past 29 years of RAGBRAI.

— Warren Taylor, photographer
The Des Moines Register

Bike ride across Iowa

By John Karras

Donald Kaul and I are going to ride from Sioux City to Davenport the week of Aug. 26 and we'd like to have as many of you as are able join us along the way.

The purpose of the trip, sponsored by our boss, The Des Moines Register and Tribune, is to promote cycling on Iowa's great cycling asset, paved secondary roads.

You're welcome to join us for a morning, a day or the entire trip. Anyone who rides with us at all will receive a certificate. Anyone completing the entire ride (please figure on making your own overnight accommodations) will receive special recognition.

We'll leave Sioux City at 8 a.m. Aug. 26 and ride to Storm Lake, about 65 miles. On the way we'll pass through such great towns as Kingsley, Washta, and Quimby.

On Aug. 27, we'll leave Storm Lake at 8 a.m. and ride to Fort Dodge, passing through Varina, Pioneer and Clare on the way. Distance about 62 miles.

The third day, Aug. 28, we'll pedal from Fort Dodge to Ames, about 65 miles, passing through Coalville, Sumner, Stratford, Boone and Luther (a rather roundabout route, but Boone and Story counties apparently have never gotten together on which roads to pave across the county line).

The fourth day, Aug. 29, is a day of rest. We'll ride from Ames to Des Moines, a mere 35 miles, with a wave at Kelley, and a salute to Slater, Sheldahl and Polk City along the way.

The fifth day, Aug. 30, will be a killer. We'll ride from Des Moines to Williamsburg – about 100 miles. The route takes us through Altoona, Mitchelville, Colfax, Prairie City, Reasnor, Sully, Lynnville, Searsboro, Montezuma, Deep River (home of the South Side Grocery Store) and Millersburg.

The last day, Aug. 31, takes us from Williamsburg to Davenport, about 85 miles. We'll pass through Iowa City, West Branch, Rochester, Moscow, Wilton Junction, Durant and Walcott.

In all, the ride will total something over 400 miles and will touch 18 counties – Woodbury, Plymouth, Cherokee, Buena Vista, Pocahontas, Humboldt, Webster, Hamilton, Boone, Story, Polk, Jasper, Poweshiek, Iowa, Johnson, Cedar, Muscatine and Scott. If any of you bicycle club people care to tie in with this ride and raise money for local bike paths or other worthwhile projects, you're certainly welcome to join in.

But whatever your purpose, please try to join us for a few glorious hours in the saddle.

We're going to ride rain or shine, hot or cold. Each day's ride will leave at 8 a.m. except the 100-miler to Williasmburg. That day, we'll leave at 7 a.m. We'll let you know about the departure points later.

See you in August.

The Des Moines Register: July 22, 1973

Donald Kaul ended up on a detour for about one mile as riders approach Sheldahl on a county road, 1973.
ʰoto by Frank Folwell

On the Road

On the road between Council Bluffs and Red Oak on the first day of RAGBRAI XIV, 1986

YOU NEVER KNOW what's going to happen on a RAGBRAI. Once you get on the road, every day is different. Every route has it's own personality. Every town is unique. Every mile brings a new adventure. The ride goes on, sweeping you along. It's best not to fight it. Go with the flow. Relax. Let things happen to you. No matter what happens, I'll be there to make pictures of the struggle, the triumph and the pain.

Even though it's always different, certain things always stay with you, like getting up early to ride into the rising sun. Stopping for a pork chop at 8:30 in the morning – breakfast was hours ago, miles ago. Whether it's a field of sunflowers or beans, or corn, or a hog lot there are sights and smells you won't forget. You can see the grain elevator of the next town in the distance. Is that a cappuccino stand at the crossroads up ahead? Let's rest here. Pancakes for lunch. A cornfield for a rest room. Give that kid a high five; he's probably slapped palms with thousands of riders already.

If you get into a groove, life is simple. The road provides everything you need. There's lots of time to think. About the wind. About the weather. About food. The music playing around you. The cute rider in front of you- with the tight shorts you've been drafting behind for the last hour.

Of course you're never really alone. It's not a race, you can't win a RAGBRAI. Thousands of riders ahead, thousands behind. Pass ten riders on the way up a hill, twenty pass you on the way down. All shapes, all sizes, all ages. Riding across Iowa from the Missouri River to the Mississippi River ... every mile is an adventure.

— Doug Wells, photographer
The Des Moines Register

▲ **John F. E. Steger, 39, of Dyersville** dips his rear bicycle wheel into the Missouri River in Dodge Park. He rode his bike to Council Bluffs from Dyersville to begin SAGBRAI, the Second Annual Great Bicycle Ride Across Iowa, 1974. *Photo by Carl Voss*

▸ **Leon Moss of Des Moines** observed by his daughters Janet, 15, and Carla, 9, backs his car carrying four bicycles into a camping place in Hawarden City Park on the eve of RAGBRAI III, 1975.

Photo by Carl Voss

Cyclists pedal into Davenport on the Great Six Day Bicycle Ride Across Iowa, which two years later became RAGBRAI. Few wore helmets then, 1973. *Photo by Carl Voss*

Donald Kaul, left, with Clarence Pickard. At age 83, the retired farmer from Indianola hadn't been on a bike for 20 years when he purchased a Schwinn to ride every mile of the Great Six-Day Bicycle Ride. *Photo by Frank Folwell*

200 Join Kaul, Karras at Start of 6-Day Bike Ride

By John Karras
(Register Staff Writer)

STORM LAKE, IA. — More than 200 riders joined Over the Coffee columnist Donald Kaul and me at the start of the Great Six-Day Bicycle Ride Across Iowa from Sioux City Sunday.

There were old and young, thin and fat, fit and flabby. Several families and hordes of lean teenagers were on the line for this 70-mile leg from Sioux City to Storm Lake.

Heat, breakdowns, and hills in the little Sioux Valley east of Sioux City took their toll, and no accurate count of how many riders finished the ride to Storm Lake was available.

But the chief inspiration of the day was provided by Clarence Pickard, a retired Indianola farmer. Pickard is 83 years old.

With the temperature reaching a high of 99 degrees, Pickard kept plugging along on his 10-speed bike, which he bought only Saturday.

"I never saw one of these bikes before this," he said. But the people he talked to pressed him to buy a 10-speed for a trip of this distance.

He hopes to ride the entire way from Sioux City to Davenport, an estimated 410 miles. Pickard said he rode a bike in high school and college but he trained only "about half a block" for this ride.

"The young person who isn't out of college yet," he said, "has no business with anything but a bicycle, no matter how much money they have."

He fell down twice during the day, he said. "Whenever I have trouble, I just go down, then get myself up kind of easy."

Why is he doing this?

"Just a fool idea I had," he said. "My wife is going into a hospital and I hadn't had any vacation so I thought I'd take a vacation."

The Des Moines Register: August 27, 1973

▲ **Carter LeBeau** of Davenport found this country stream too good to pass up as he pedaled his way toward Cherokee, 1982. *Photo by Carl Voss*

Applaud, Honor Bikers At End of Six-Day Ride

By Larry Eckholt
(Register Staff Writer)

DAVENPORT, IA — The Great Six-Day Bike Ride came to a festive conclusion Friday at Davenport's Vander Veer park, with the bicyclists congratulating each other for their perseverance and many onlookers questioning their sanity.

And, yes – Clarence Pickard made it.

More than 100 bikers who set out from Sioux City on Sunday were joined by an estimated 150 other area cyclists at the outskirts of Davenport late Friday afternoon.

The procession of bikes continued to grow as it pedaled its way through the city's rush-hour traffic. At the park, Davenport Mayor Kathryn Kirschbaum presentred The Register's John Karras with a certificate of merit and congratulated the bikers for their success.

The Register's Donald Kaul was still en route to the park at the time of the festivities, keeping an eye on the amazing Mr. Pickard, 83, who at the time was still 10 miles out of town, but nearing the end of his six-day, 460-mile odyssey.

Indianola's Mr. Pickard – who has made a silver pith helmet into a new symbol of virility and longevity – arrived at the park about 7 p.m. to the applause of some 100 well-wishers who had waited since the arrival of the main pack of riders.

He was presented a "Super Senior Citizen of the Day" certificate by Mayor Kirschbaum. Kaul, who rode in with Pickard, received a "cerificate of merit" from the mayor.

Pickard rolled up his certificate, stuck it in a shirt pocket and proceeded with the business of signing autographs, shaking hands and answering questions.

Everywhere between Williamsburg and Davenport, Iowans had come out in droves to greet Mr. Pickard.

At the western edge of Iowa City, students from Ernest Horn Elementary School lined the street with outreached hands to touch the passing Mr. Pickard. "here he comes in the silver helmet," yelled one youngster.

In West Branch, Mr. Pickard was met by Terry Alliband, 29, a University of Iowa graduate student who served in the Peace Corps with Pickard and his wife in India in 1966-1968. Alliband and his wife, Ruth, went through Peace Corps training with Pickard and his wife Mildred.

"He was wearing his pith helmet then, too," said Alliband. "He was phenomenal, the way he could relate to young people."

An 18-year-old Dubuque biker, Bill Wertzburger, who pedaled his bicycle from Dubuque to Sioux City to join the bicycling expedition, decided to become Pickard's riding partner Friday, and the two talked for miles about each other's experiences. "He's really interesting to talk to," said Wertzburger. "He knows a lot about just about everything."

The Des Moines Register: September 1, 1973

◄◄ **Rider and Riders,** 1982, between Tipton and Independence.
Photo by Harry Baumert

◄ **A rider hoists her** bike as she completes RAGBRAI at Burlington, 1979.
Photo by Larry E. Neibergall

▼ **Before email** and cell phones there was the very popular phone booth.
Photo by David Lewis

◀ **A jubilant Mim Romero** catches sight of her husband, Ben, nearing the end of RAGBRAI IX in Keokuk. She was so excited she forgot to take his picture, and gave him a hug instead. The Romeros came to Iowa from Las Vegas, Nevada, to join thousands of bikers for RAGBRAI. *Photo by David Peterson*

◀▾ **Nashua farmer** Kirk Bailey follows riders on his way to wind row oats, 1982. *Photo by Harry Baumert*

▾ **Hitching a ride**, 1982. *Photo by Harry Baumert*

▾▾ **Corn stalk** on the ride from Hawarden to Sibley, 1985. *Photo by Gary Fandel*

▲ **Leaving Sioux City**, 1988. *Photo by Doug Wells*

◀ **On the road** again, 1986. *Photo by Loup Langton*

▶ **Clowning around** somewhere between Storm Lake and Fort Dodge, 1987.

Photo by Bill Neibergall

◄◄ **Last stop for** RAGBRAI XIX, Bellevue, 1991. *Photo by Harry Baumert*

◄ **Another RAGBRAI** comes to an end, Bellevue, 1989. *Photo by Terry Farris*

▼ **John Maniscalco** of San Francisco, California, right, hugs his partner, Bob Rienecker, also of San Francisco, after both rode their bicycles off a Mississippi dock to celebrate the end of RAGBRAI in Burlington. Rain made the last day difficult. But Maniscalco said he didn't mind the conditions. "I don't care. I'll do this ride till I die," 1990. *Photo by Jeffrey Z. Carney*

▶ **With a long** downhill run and a northwest tailwind to boot, RAGBRAI XIX riders scoot down Highway 206 entering the west edge of Lacona where residents had the town decked out in flags and plenty of refreshments on hand. *Photo by Robert Nandell*

▸ A bicyclist answers nature's call in a cornfield along the road between Marion and Maquoketa, 1994. *Photo by Harry Baumert*

▾ Riders at the finish of RAGBRAI XXII in Clinton, 1994. *Photo by Harry Baumert*

Men's
Rest Room ↑

▲ **Corn stalks and local folk** along the route from Council Bluffs to Harlan, 1994.
Photo by Doug Wells

▸ **Karen Littman,** 27, left, checks in with her boss in New York via cellular phone during a break in Colwell, 1996. She is a health care consultant.
Photo by Harry Baumert

A patch of flowers greets riders west of oralville on the last day of RAGBRAI XXIII, 1995. *noto by Harry Baumert*

Cyclists and a horse and buggy roll along ide-by-side on the road into Moravia during AGBRAI XXIII. *Photo by Amanda Saslow*

A wave of RAGBRAI riders passes a sea of corn n route to Northwood on a morning ride, 1996. *noto by Harry Baumert*

◄◄**Jim Newbold** of Chicago, Illinois, returns to his bicycle after a satisfying plunge in the Mississippi River in Ft. Madison, the final stop of RAGBRAI XXIV. *Photo by Harry Baumert*

◄ **Riders near** Pittsburg maneuver a curve while climbing a hill, 1997. *Photo by Harry Baumert*

▶ **Riders pass over** the Des Moines River at the Keosauqua bridge heading out of town, 1997.
Photo by Harry Baumert

▼ **On the fourth day** of RAGBRAI XXV, 10,000 bicyclists rode from Des Moines to Chariton. On the way they passed through Indianola, Lacona and Oakley. Some of the riders zoom past signs put up by the proud citizens of Milo. *Photo by Harry Baumert*

SPEED ZONE AHEAD

IS THIS HEAVEN?

NO, IT'S MILO!

◄ **A bike of hay bales** made a great stop for cyclists to take a picture at a rest station in Underwood during RAGBRAI XXV. *Photo by Sher Stoneman*

◄▾ **A RAGBRAI cyclist** rides past two balloons in Indianola, 1997. Early fog kept the balloons, a reminder that the National Balloon Classic was being held there the same day, on the ground. *Photo by Kevin Wolf*

▾ **A banana peel** is left along the road near Roland as riders roll by, 1998. Bananas are a favorite among riders. *Photo by Sher Stoneman*

▸ **Two RAGBRAI riders** get on the road early in the morning, 1998. These two were a few miles out of Farnhamville by 7 a.m. *Photo by Tina Yee*

▾ **Sabula RAGBRAI** Committee co-chair Al Mangler and recording secretary Sandra Kempter exchanged their pedals for paddles for this photo. RAGBRAI XXVI finished in Sabula, Iowa's only island town. Of course, cyclists got there by causeway rather than canoe. *Photo by Harry Baumert*

◀ **Arlene Yoder** of Williamsburg and her sister Cindy Carter of Blue Grass hug and cry after dipping their front tires in the Mississippi River at the end of RAGBRAI XXVI in Sabula. *Photo by Tina Yee*

▼ **Riders pass** the towers of a wind farm south of Clear Lake, 1999. *Photo by Doug Wells*

◄ **Steve Dudak,** an Iowa State Patrol trooper, swigs water as he and retired farmer Claire Schnor rest in the shade of Dudak's patrol car hood south of Sumner, 1999. The open hood provided shade and helped keep the idling engine from overheating. *Photo by Harry Baumert*

◄▼ **At Crystal Lake, 1999,** some of the members of the Cruisin' Californians from the bay area, take a breather. *Photo by Gary Fandel*

▼ **When you're tired,** even concrete makes a good bed, as long as it's in the shade. Greg O'Grady of Des Moines catches a nap at a mid-day stop in West Union, 1999. *Photo by Harry Baumert*

▼▼ **Bob Perry** of Des Moines sweeps gravel on a turn in the route at Elgin after watching some fellow riders wipe out, 1999. *Photo by Bob Modersohn*

▲ **Matthew Baldwin,** 10, shades himself from the sun north of West Union as he hawks lemonade and homemade doughnuts, which his family was selling, 1999. *Photo by Harry Baumert*

◄ **Riders wait** for a train to pass before leaving Fort Atkinson, 1999. *Photo by Harry Baumert*

▼ **Third day of RAGBRAI XXVII,** Algona to Clear Lake. Just east of Algona, a State Trooper directs bikers across Hwy 18 early in the morning, 1999. *Photo by Gary Fandel*

On the third day of RAGBRAI XXVII, an ultralight plane flys over bikers ear Hayfield, 1999. *Photo by Doug Wells*

Randy Karon, of Barrington, Illinois, handles three cameras to photoaph friends as they dip their bike wheels in the Mississippi at end of de, 1999. *Photo by Harry Baumert*

Onlookers: "Watching the muscles go by," remarked Lawrence hetstine as he and his wife, Louise, watched riders pass the junction of ashington County roads W38 and G38, 2000. *Photo by Bob Modersohn*

RAGBRAI riders had the chance to stop at the one-store burg of Dub- along G38 in Washington County, 2000. *Photo by Bob Modersohn*

▶ **Jennifer Lennon**, 26, of Marshall, Michigan, hugs her grandparents, Bette and Roger Coulson of Ames good-bye as she heads back onto the route. Lennon grew up in Rockford. Her grandparents had come down and parked at the corner of E63 and R38 outside Slater waiting to see if they'd see her when she went by, 2001. *Photo by Tina Yee*

▼ **Trooper Norm Buenger** directs bicycle traffic northeast of Ottumwa during RAGBRAI XXVIII. *Photo by Harry Baumert*

▼▼ **RAGBRAI riders** pass Wapello County Grain Company near Agency, 2000. *Photo by Harry Baumert*

◀ **Joel Alberts,** of Minneapolis, Minnesota, left and Joe Hedinger, of Cleveland, Ohio, walk into the Mississippi River at Muscatine after completing RAGBRAI XXIX, 2001. Alberts, born and raised in Sanborn and Hedinger, originally from Paullina, were first-time riders.
Photo by Harry Baumert

▼ **Andy Wolter,** 5, of Perry takes aim to greet a RAGBRAI rider rolling past his house during RAGBRAI XXIV.
Photo by Gary Fandel

The Hills

Climbing a hill between Killduff and Oakland Acres, 1991.
Photo by Warren Taylor

IF I ONLY HAD A DIME for every time I heard a RAGBRAI rider say, "I thought Iowa was flat," well I'd have a pocketful of dimes.

It seems most new riders think Iowa is flatter than a Chris Cake, probably based on one of the two interstate highways criss-crossing the state. Usually the first 15 miles on the first day of the ride reveal Iowa's rolling hills, I think even veteran riders are still amazed at some of the hills here. It's not that riders aren't warned, if they have a chance to read some articles on preparing for the ride. When RAGBRAI co-founder John Karras isn't preaching the benefits of wearing a helmet (he was especially hard on 'Team Hair' one year) he's warning riders to log some of those training miles on the hills.

Iowa is anything but flat. The Loess Hills at the beginning, especially if you are heading into their teeth north of Council Bluffs, are more likely to raise a rider's heart rate than an advancing thunderstorm from the west. Iowa has folds, Iowa undulates, and it follows the paths of long ago glaciers that came to rest here. Farmers, who spent decades trying to lay the fields flat, have learned to co-exist with the sudden rises and falls of the supine landscape.

And the hills, things that rise and fall gently when you're in an air conditioned car on the highway, are at times daunting when your only forward motion relies on two tired legs. Add a head wind and one of those daring storms that spring up from the fields on a hot August afternoon and a rider can feel the need for a Sherpa.

— Gary Fandel, photographer
The Des Moines Register

▲ **Some walked,** some rode to get up the challenging hill between Sigourney and Mt. Pleasant during the 1975 ride
Photo by Warren Taylor

◄ **Tribune reporter** Bob Hullihan, left, interviews exausted riders at the top of Waterworks Hill west of Boone, 1975. *Photo by George Ceolla*

▲ **Riders work** their way up a hill near Red Oak, 1976. *Photo by David Lewis*

◀◀ **A hill to climb** outside of Sioux City, 1978. *Photo by Larry E. Neibergall*

◀ **Walking the bike** up a steep hill near Farrar, 1975. *Photo by Warren Taylor*

▼ **Walking was the method** of choice to get up Waterworks Hill near Boone during the 1975 ride. *Photo by Warren Taylor*

Bike crusade's towering legend: 'The Hill

By Robert Hullihan

The 10-speed crusaders rode into Jerusalem Saturday. It looked a lot like Fort Madison and the end of the third Great Bicycle Ride across Iowa – RAGBRAI III.

But to the knights-of-the-narrow saddle, who pedaled 450 miles from Hawarden to get to the Mississippi River town, it was another place and another time.

It was the mythical city that had beckoned them on through six days of quest overland turned magical with lemonade stands and little country churches offering ham sandwiches.

And it was a time when the riders were no longer plumbers, students, salesmen, housewives, farmers, bureaucrats or computer programmers.

In their straggling hundreds they became one toiling body with an aching bottom, sunburned nose and a scent of insect repellent.

And they were going to Jerusalem together on their faithful Fujis, Schwinns, Seraph Sprees, Brownings, Gitanes, Falcons, Bianchis and Vistas.

It was six days suspended between past and future. They were all half in love with one another and with the people who stood in small towns and farmyards to wave them on.

So, when they rode into Fort Madison Saturday, they hosannaed in the streets and wagged their little red and yellow pennants through town to delay the discharge of their gentle army.

They looked at one another and knew that nothing ever would be the same again. Not quite. They shouted promises and dispersed to become plumbers and programmers once more – and to fashion the legends of RAGBRAI III.

Waterworks Hill just west of Boone will tower in the legends.

It's the place where The Great Bicycle Ride first became The Great Bicycle Walk last Tuesday afternoon for most of the jolly pedalers in motley.

The RAGBRAI band did a softshoe shuffle on "THE HILL" and the host came struggling up on foot for hours out of the Des Moines River Valley.

They walked in long, penitent lines, pushing their bicycles along like bright, frail sins come to judgment. They came bunched in consolation. They talked together in low-gear:

"Well, it wouldn't have made me a better human being," said one woman, looking back down the hill

she had failed to pedal.

"My bicycle seat is critical," explained another. "It's like four G Streets end to end," panted Geneva Hiveley of Fort Dodge. "A wonderful hill! A work of beauty! A beast!" gasped Don Bates, 44, a salesman from Davenport. He remounted the Fuji Racer that he had pushed up the hill and rode on to "a Nupercainal night in Boone."

Walt Anderson, 55, of Fort Dodge, reclined in a shady ditch watching RAGBRAI limp past, stripped to its soul.

Still, among them rode a few bearers of the flame: The young, the strong, the proud, the foolish.

Faith under torture

These pedaled to the top of the hill with expressions of fanatics who refuse to give up the faith under torture. And they began the legend.

"Three-mile hill! one kid gulped, as he pumped to the top.

Within 20 minutes another kid made it and rasped: "Four-mile hill!"

See how it works? There were riders that day who will tell grandchildren about "Ten-mile hill at Boone."

Since it is important to keep the record straight in matters of the embattled spirit, it should be known that Waterworks Hill is only one-half mile long.

But it rises as steeply as a utility bill.

Rita Efta, "THE taxidermist from Auburn," said it was the first hill she ever has had to walk on a bicycle ride.

She looked around at bicyclists sprawled in shade at the top of the hill as though judging which one would look best mounted on someone's wall.

Rita rode on into Boone without selecting a specimen.

Arnie Waldstein, 50, a farm manger from Storm Lake, walked up the hill, his bicycle seat lumpy with a chunk of unavailing foam rubber.

"A taste of the free life," he grinned, taking a place in the ditch.

"Agony, ecstasy"

Alan Christensen, 50, a social worker from Des Moines, pushed his bike up the hill to speak ennobling words: "This is the agony," he said. "The ecstasy comes in Fort Madison – the completion."

It seemed proper sentiment for crusaders.

But there were times, as bikers and walkers littered the top of Waterworks Hill, when RAGBRAI looked

as through it had just been defeated by the Turks.

Steve Dickey, a 22-year-old plumber from Packwood, pedaled all the way up, flopped in the ditch, and judged himself "stupid to try it. I lost my wife and sister down there."

Mary Dickey finally came walking up the grade. "Is that you?" said Steve, through a haze of sweat.

"It is not me," said Mary, taking her place in the ditch.

Known as Bikini

There was a stir among the watchers on the hilltop. "Hey here comes Bikini!" She's making it. She's making it. Oh, wow!"

A spectacular young woman pedaled past, her tongue hanging out in exhaustion. She will forever be known in RAGBRAI legend by the bathing suit she wore. The "wow" was well spoken.

"She's caused more wrecks!" hissed a woman from the ditch. Even crusaders aren't perfect.

But the mood was one of almost overwhelming goodwill. Everyone who got to the top of the hill, whether afoot, or astride a bike, was beautiful and worthy to everyone else.

Except, perhaps, for the punk kid who did a wheelie (a wheelie!) right below the crest. "Only way to climb a hill," he yelled to the gallery in the ditch.

Taiwon Kim, 14, of Marshalltown, pedaled straight up the hill then sat there astride his bike, like a sentinel. He was waiting for Anne Roberts, 18, of Des Moines to ride up the grade.

"Oh, she'll make it. It ruins the whole trip if you walk up a hill," he said, sternly, Anne made it pedaling all the way.

Mutual self-esteem

"That really helped my self-esteem," she gasped. "Taiwon talks me into it. He just uses positive words: You can do it!" You can do it!"

In the constantly shifting neighborhoods of the bike ride, Anne and Taiwon were pedaling companions for the day. They rode on into Boone glowing with mutual esteem.

Harley Van Dyke, 74, and a sheep-shearer from Vinton, walked up the hill, "to get the charlie horses out of my legs."

Luckily, Harley had gone on before Leon Pearson came up. Leon was looking a bit sheepish, wearing one of his wife's laced and flowered shirts.

"It's for the sunburn," explained the 49-year-old medical technician

from Omaha. "No one has attacked me yet, but some of them are startir to smile at me." Leon rode on, looing stunning.

Behind him walked a farmer wearing bib overalls and fancy, Italian bicycle racing shoes. A youn woman came by in a cutoff Mother Hubbard.

At mid-afternoon, word came that a man was pedaling up the hill, pumping to a horse chant:

"God Damn Karras; God Damn Kaul."God Damn Karras: God Dar Kaul.

Well it is widely known that crusaders often call upon the saints in time of need. (Yes, Karras and Kau each made it up the hill late in the day. But it was a near thing.)

Steve Schares, 24, from Dubuqu paused at the top of the hill and handed his canteen of water to Nan Dykstra of Hull. He told how it wa on The Great Bicycle Ride:

"Really a mellow time. A lot of brotherhood. It's so nice to go fron town to town and talk to all the peo ple. How great the people are.

Nancy, 24, handed the canteen back to Steve and climbed on her bicycle again after walking up Waterworks Hill. "Ungracefully, I enter town," she said, and pedaled c toward Boone.

Young Brenndan Riddles of Ced Rapids came booming up the hill to the tune of "Rhinestone Cowboy" o his transistor radio.

A green-eyed 13-year-old with yellow hair cut in a page boy, he stood looking back down at the line of marchers, like Prince Valiant con to rally the rear guard.

He claimed to be living off the land: "Mostly lemonade and the fre stuff. I've come too far to stop," he yelled, leaping on his bike and peda ing off in a cloud of music:

"…And nice guys get washed away like the snow and the rain…"

All afternoon the long line of walkers pushed bikes up the hill, pennants waving over empty saddle But the spirit moved among them. They were all saved in one another.

Kathy Hughes, 13, from Storm Lake, paused among the RAGBRAI column struggling over the crest.

"And now I have to go to the bathroom," she said. "Wouldn't yo know?"

Scholars will tell you that these very words have been spoken in all the languages of man at critical moments in every crusade in the his tory of the world.

Even on the road to Jerusalem.

The Des Moines Register: August 10, 1975

John Karras on his bike in Mt. Hosmer City Park at Lansing. Much of the hill leading to this spectacular Mississippi River overlook is at an 18 percent grade, 1990. *Photo by Harry Baumert*

RAGBRAI riders cruise along Iowa's rolling hills leading into Prescott during RAGBRAI XXV, 1997. *Photo by Sher Stoneman*

Cyclists form a long, squiggly line as they pedal up and down hills along County Road L56 just after sunrise a few miles north of Quimby, 1998.
Photo by Sher Stoneman

Hillary LaVoie of Monroe, Wisconsin, catches a quick nap in Prescott after conquering the hills into town, 1997.
Photo by Amanda Saslow

Riders crest a hill on the way from Russian to West Union, 1999 and are greeted by an Iowa skyline.
Photo by Harry Baumert

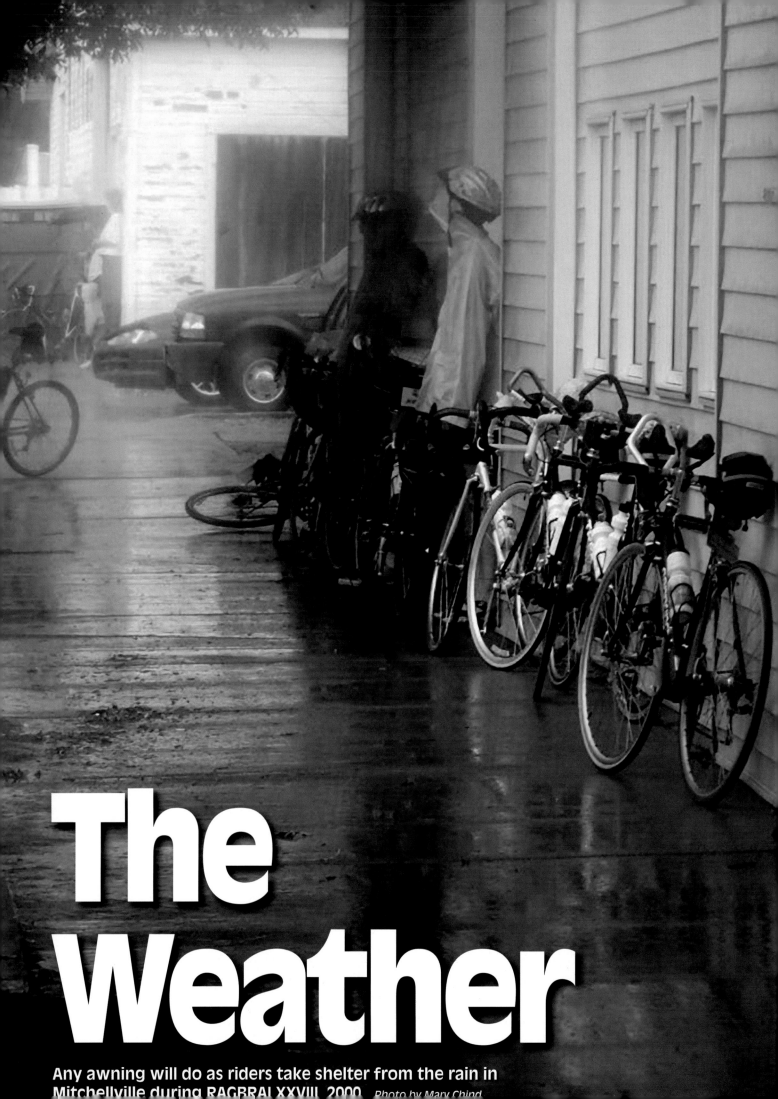

The Weather

Any awning will do as riders take shelter from the rain in Mitchellville during RAGBRAI XXVIII, 2000. *Photo by Mary Chind*

SUNSHINE AND RAIN are the friend and enemy to the photographer. Fortunately I can take cover from the elements in-between focusing on the riders passing by on a hot, muggy day.

Sunscreen and ponchos are a good idea, but let's face it; no amount of preparation can totally protect riders from the wrath of Mother Nature. Whatever conditions she brings, they are shared experience and become the topic of conversation at any porta potty line or campsite along the route. Rain or winds can leave riders feeling at their worst but can sometimes bring out their best. Although we may not believe it at the time, the added challenge of dealing with Mother Nature has a way of uniting us and bringing out our good sides and our sense of humor. Maybe it's better to laugh than to cry in some of those situations.

It is not so strange that these bad weather rides can bring out the best in riders, although they may be feeling at their worst. The added challenge of dealing with Mother Nature unites us and brings out our good side and our sense of humor. Maybe it's better to laugh than to cry in some of those situations. Whatever the real answer is, many veteran riders agree that some of their most memorable rides were due to adverse weather conditions.

When the weather makes obstacles for riders I'm happy to be on the side of the road making images. I've watched the RAGBRAI faithful grimace and grumble through strong headwinds. I've lain in a ditch as noisy wheels slipped into early morning fog. A fake snowball has hit me. I've laughed with riders taking cover from the rain as we watched the plastic fashion show whizzing by. When I'm cold or wet like they are I'm thankful I'm not on two wheels myself, but then I know I'm not experiencing it for real.

— Mary Chind, photographer
The Des Moines Register

▲ A soggy RAGBRAI rider splashes out of a night's camping stop at Pella. A steady downpour greeted riders but gradually eased as they pedaled on to Ottumwa, 1984. *Photo by Warren Taylor*

◄◄ Sunblock is essential for RAGBRAI participants, young and old. Two youngsters receive sunblock during the 1976 ride near Muscatine. *Photo by Frank Folwell*

◄ Joyce Bricker of Stratford applies sunblock before setting out on the next leg, 1982.
Photo by Harry Baumert

KAUL

Over the coffee®

MAPLETON, IA. — Okay God, I'm sorry. I apologize for saying You're untrustworthy. It was just a dumb joke. I didn't mean it.

You're not going to hold it against me and make the rest of the week like the first day of this miserable ride, are You? You're too big for that. I promise not to do it again.

I don't know how to explain the first day of RAGBRAI IX except in terms of Divine Retribution. It was awful.

First of all, it rained; not a lot, but enough. Enough to make one's clothes all wet. Biking in the rain poses certain problems. If you put on a slicker, in hopes of staying dry, you sweat a lot, getting wet from the inside. Then, when you take off the slicker, the wind generated by biking chills you. This is especially true when it's cold, and it was cold Sunday. Again, not very cold, but it is the end of July after all.

It was cold enough. Biking in the cold and wet is, I suspect, not unlike the feeling 19th century mental patients experienced when orderlies at institutions would wrap them in cold, wet sheets in an attempt to calm them. It didn't work then, it doesn't work now.

But the cold and wet could be said to have been the best things about RAGBRAI Sunday. The worst was the wind. All day long, without cease, we bucked a 20 mph headwind. I don't know why I say 20. It could have been 30. All I know is that my water bottle had white caps on it.

Biking into a strong headwind is one of the worst kinds of biking. You hear people complain about hills, but hills make a bike ride interesting. Hills have an upside, but they also have a downside, when you can bend low over the handlebars and go lickety-split.

There is no downside to a headwind.

A headwind sucks your strength like a wolf sucks the bone marrow of a lamb. You crouch low, trying to make yourself into an approximation of a bullet and the back of your neck begins to hurt. Eventually it feels like someone's driven a knife into your back, just above the shoulder blades.

Then your knees begin to complain. Mine are complaining right now. They're telling me; "You jerk. Who needs this schlepping across Iowa once a year. If you're going to do this, you have to give us more practice."

And Sunday was supposed to be the easy day on the ride, a day to break the riders in to the ordeal gradually. Some easy day. Another like it and I'll be eligible for worker's compensation.

It happens like this every year. I forget how hard RAGBRAI is. People like John Karras will tell you that it's no big deal, that anyone can do it. Don't believe them.

RAGBRAI, except for the young, except for the inordinately conditioned, is a trial. Biking 60 to 100 miles a day for a week in the rain and heat and cold against the wind is difficult work.

The lucky ones fall off their bicycles and get hurt. They get to rest in the hospital. The rest of us have to press on, just as though we were having a good time.

I am at a loss to explain why we do it. Oh, I used to say, glibly, that people responded to the challenge of it, but I'm not sure that's true. Everything about life is a challenge. You don't have to hurt all over in order to feel superior.

I think, perhaps, the answer might be found on the dark side of human nature. I think RAGBRAI might satisfy the sado-masochistic urges of people who aren't into leather.

That's not totally fair. There is a more positive side to the ride. There is a sense of community about it, a shared experience which is rare in contemporary life.

There is a reality to it. You're not watching other people do something, you're doing something yourself. In a society that seems to be suffocating in vicarious experience, even pain can be a virtue.

But back to God.

He did not deal the ride a complete bust hand on Sunday. It was a 52-mile ride. The first 49 were as I have described them – grueling, arduous, painful. For the last three miles into Mapleton, however, He arranged a glorious downhill swoop.

Exhausted, wondering whether you could go on, you were allowed the delicious experience of lying down over your bike and zooming into town as though you were on the Tour de France. It was an exquisite experience.

Perhaps that means He's forgiven me for not trusting Him. I trust that is so. If not, I may not finish out the week.

The Des Moines Register: July 27, 1981

▲▲ **Riding through the rain** north of Iowa City during RAGBRAI XVIII, 1990.
Photo by Jeffrey Z. Carney

▲ **Kayo Aslagson** of Starbuck, Minnesota, puts on his rain gear in Stuart, 2000.
Photo by Doug Wells

So how close did RAGBRAI-XXI come to being canceled?

Iowa Boy
Chuck Offenburger

SIOUX CITY, IA. — As 8,000 cyclists from around the world gather here today for the start on Sunday of RAGBRAI-XXI, one hot topic of conversation is bound to be how close the big bike ride came to being canceled in this year of devastating flooding in Iowa.

Well?

The idea was seriously considered for several hours on July 12 and 13 by top executives of the sponsoring Des Moines Register, but "I don't think we actually got very close to calling it off," said Diane Glass, vice-president of marketing.

"My primary concern was whether the event would be jeopardizing the safety of people, and with this northern Iowa route, that didn't seem to be a problem," she continued. "And a big reason for going ahead was that the host communities already had made such significant investments in RAGBRAI coming. We figure the economic impact of RAGBRAI happening in Iowa for a week is about $2 million, so canceling would have really hurt the state."

Register publisher Charlie Edwards said the company "touched base with the governor's office because state government is so involved in RAGBRAI with the State Patrol and economic development and tourism. We wanted to find out what they thought about having the event when the whole state is a disaster area."

"We got a resounding 'yes' from the state that we should go ahead," Edwards continued. "They said if there's anything Iowans really need right now, it's a positive message that life goes on -- that we still can and should celebrate.

"We went ahead and checked then with each of the overnight communities on the RAGBRAI route, and each of them said yes, let's do it. So it seemed to be pretty clear we should go ahead."

Edwards, who has ridden RAGBRAI in past years but won't this summer, shook his head thinking about it. "It tells you something about the importance of RAGBRAI to this company and to this state," he said, "that at the most critical time in this company's history – when we were focusing on the very basics of whether we were going to be able to publish a paper and arranging portable toilets and getting food and water – we took time to make decisions about RAGBRAI.

"It's so important to this state in terms of our psyche, our feelings about community and about community spirit. So much of RAGBRAI is almost spiritual, and anybody who's been on it understands that. Now was not the time, with all the tragedy in this state, to cancel an event that says so much about our spirit."

Remember droughts? Don Benson, retired Register public relations director and for 19 years coordinator of RAGBRAI, said the only time there was mention of canceling the ride in his years "was one time in the early '80s in exactly the opposite situation as now – a drought. We were concerned what impact our 8,000 people would have on the water supplies of towns, but the towns all said they could handle it, and they did." In the grim farm crisis years of the mid-'80s, he said, "some people might have thought RAGBRAI should be canceled, but not the people out in the towns along the way. They looked on RAGBRAI as the one bright spot in those summers. I think it will be kind of like that this summer, too."

The Des Moines Register: July 24, 1993

▶ **Steve Smartt** of Nashville, Tennessee, plays "Stormy Weather" on his horn at 6:15 a.m. in Chariton, 1997. It was a fitting wake-up call since a thunderstorm passed over the area overnight.
Photo by Harry Baumert

An early thunderstorm soaked the RAGBRAI campground in Red Oak during RAGBRAI XXV. Despite the lightning and ownpour, many riders decided to get an early start - and got soaked. *Photo by Amanda Saslow*

Some nights in the campgrounds are more interesting than others, 1997. *Photo by Amanda Saslow*

▲ **Irene Knickerbocker,** 31, of Radcliffe cools off in a water spray set up for RAGBRAI riders entering Hawkeye, 1996. *Photo by Harry Baumert*

▸ **Shala Burtsfield** of Liberal, Kansas, shows off her bike rider's sunburn in Spencer, 1999. *Photo by Doug Wells*

▾ **Six-year-old Clayton Woodke** sprays RAGBRAI riders as they enter Schaller, 1998. *Photo by Tina Yee*

◄▲ Mary Swanstrom of Dalton, Minnesota, cools off in a water tank near Washta, 2001. *Photo by Carl Voss*

▲ Factory worker Melissa Morris, 16, spends part of her lunch break helping RAGBRAI riders on their way through Keosauqua cool off in the sweltering heat, 1997. *Photo by Harry Baumert*

◄ Brad Cronk of Iowa City washes the mud off his bike after dipping his tires in the Big Sioux River, 1998. *Photo by Sher Stoneman*

◄▼ A RAGBRAIer reacts to the cool shower he received from a sprinkler set up over the road into Chariton by a kindly couple, 1997. *Photo by Amanda Saslow*

▼ Jerry Harbison, 14, a RAGBRAI rider from Germany, takes a more drastic approach to cooling off at Crystal Lake, 1999. *Photo by Gary Fandel*

▸ **Megan Kuennen,** 11, gives a brief respite to Chris Caligiuri of Des Moines as the RAGBRAI biker passes her Fort Atkinson home, 1999.
Photo by Harry Baumert

▾ **RAGBRAI riders** slow down for a water spray in George, 1999.
Photo by Doug Wells

▲ **Dieter Sturm** of Sturm Special Effects, Lake Geneva, Wisconsin, sprays manufactured snow onto a volleyball field as part of Ankeny's welcoming celebration for RAGBRAI, 2000. *Photo by Mary Chind*

◄ **Mandy Beason** of Ankeny backs up Gus Plummer of the Tall Dog Bike Club during a snow volleyball game in Ankeny, 2000. *Photo by Mary Chind*

▼ **Players struggle** to stay upright on Ankeny's snow-covered volleyball court, 2000. *Photo by Mary Chind*

Rain plays game with riders' apparel

RAGBRAI NOTES
Richard Doak

IDA GROVE, IA. – Riding bicycles in the rain is a guessing game. We had plenty of opportunity to try our guessing skills Monday morning coming out of Storm Lake on the way to Denison.

The day dawned with a steady, light rain that left campers wrestling with wet tents and soggy gear as they got under way. Hardly anyone on RAGBRAI lets a little rain stop them. After all, we're supposed to be out here enjoying nature in all its forms.

Mary Lou and I carry $5 plastic rain suits in our bike bags for just such occasions. Many others follow the RAGBRAI tradition of simply using a plastic garbage bag.

That's where the guessing comes in. When it starts to rain, if you put your plastic on too soon and the rain tapers off, you end up sweating inside a plastic suit – getting more wet from the sweat than from the rain. If you wait too long to put on the suit, and the rain intensifies, you're drenched before you can get it on.

We spent Monday morning putting the rain suits on, then taking them off, usually at the wrong times. We would get wet and cold, put on the suits to get warm, and then end up taking them off to cool off.

Another fact of riding a bicycle in the rain is that as much water kicks up from the road as falls from the sky. Your legs become covered with black road grime and your shoes become soaked through, so that you walk around all day in squishy socks.

It stopped raining often enough, however, to partake of the traditional RAGBRAI enjoyments and small-town hospitality.

Coming into Schaller, we found that Iowa is not all pork chops and pancakes. There were egg rolls, courtesy of Vilma Woodke, a native of the Philippines. She said she was up all night making more than 700 egg rolls and her homemade sweet-and-sour sauce.

Vilma said she was supposed to set up in a small park on the edge of Schaller's business district, but with the rain she moved just inside the big overhead doors of Woodke Machine Shop, operated by her husband, Scott. There you could have a breakfast egg roll for $1 amid the big metal lathes and other machinery.

Scott said he met Vilma in the Philippines, where she was an ambulance driver and he was a Marine on R & R from Vietnam. The burly machinist said he was one of the last Marines out of Saigon during the war.

He came home to work in the shop in Schaller, which had been started by his father when he returned from his own military service.

So at the edge of the Schaller business district is a two-generation business with a new partner from the Philippines. Those are the kinds of people you meet in small-town Iowa.

Farther up the street, there was free popcorn, fittingly since Schaller bills itself as the popcorn capital of the world. There was also the traditional pancakes.

Then it was on to Galva to top off breakfast with cherry pie from the lovely city park right on the RAGBRAI route. Then it was on to Ida Grove. The rain stopped. And it started to get hot.

It felt like a real RAGBRAI.

The Des Moines Register: July 24, 2001

▲ **Lauren Wright** of Columbus, Indiana, finds a dry place in a crowded tent for breakfast during a rainy stop in Schaller, 2001. *Photo by Doug Wells*

▸ **Bill George** and Ferris Wharton of Wilmington, Delaware, lean their bikes against a wall as they prepare to wait out an approaching storm in a tavern in Farnhamville, 1998. *Photo by Sher Stoneman*

◄ **Members of Team Tutu** seek shelter from the rain in Quimby during RAGBRAI XXIX. The riders were heading to Storm Lake.
Photo by Doug Wells

▼ **A lone rider** heads toward the sun on the way to Hancock on the first day of RAGBRAI XXV.
Photo by Amanda Saslow

The Equipment

Brian Finkle, Fort Collins, Colorado, adds a horn to his bicycle at the RAGBRAI campground in Missouri Valley, 1997. Photo by Sher Stoneman

THERE ARE AS MANY WAYS TO TRAVEL on RAGBRAI as there are methods of skinning the proverbial cat, probably more. From front wheel to rear axle and from headgear to biking shoes, the variety of equipment and personal accessories seems endless.

Most in the crowd of spokes and wheels take a conventional approach, wearing comfortable clothing and a standard helmet while riding a multi-speed bicycle. However, brilliant flashes of individuality accent the riding horde.

If this event were a race, all entrants would opt for speed. Some cyclists do leave early each morning, stay ahead of the pack and arrive early at the overnight destination. Their equipment: fast, light, streamlined.

A desire to display style while having fun seems to be the motivation of others, even at the cost of increased weight and wind resistance.

How else to explain the occasional daring soul atop a high wheeler, an old-time cycle with enormous front wheel and small rear wheel? Or, how about the handful of cyclists each year riding heavy old steel-framed, balloon-tired bikes with coaster brakes? One such vehicle sported the message "Ten speeds are for wimps."

It's a mystery how some riders can negotiate hills, considering what they have in tow. Dogs have ridden with their human companions and bulky stereo systems with sizeable speakers have been pulled behind. One rider, pulling a trailer with a canoe, seemed well prepared to take a break from pedaling if a lake along the route beckoned.

Some people have negotiated the flow of vehicles wearing in-line skates - tough going on gravel, no doubt - and an occasional horseman on a galloping horse has kept pace with riders for at least a few miles.

Recumbent models, with the rider in a half supine position, have become popular, as have tandem bicycles, with two, three or more passengers. Whole families sit atop one long frame. Some disabled riders, lacking use of their legs, move their vehicles with arm power, working pedals mounted high and in front. It's another example of the human spirit overcoming obstacles.

Helmets often are transformed into whimsical ornaments, displaying foam watermelon slices, pig snouts, Spam cans, deer antlers and any number of other objects.

Built for speed? Heck no. But style? You bet!

— Harry Baumert, photographer
The Des Moines Register

▲ **Lost in a sea of bikes,** RAGBRAI III, between Sigourney and Mt. Pleasant, 1975. *Photo by Frank Folwell*

◄ **Fixing a flat** during RAGBRAI IX, 1981. *Photo by Rick Rickman*

◄ **Brad Lewis** of Storm Lake runs into some trouble at Ida Grove during RAGBRAI V, 1977. Photo by Jim Selzer

▲ A vintage bike draws attention during RAGBRAI VI, 1978.
Photo by David Lewis

◄ Most RAGBRAI X riders rode on two wheels, but 24-year-old Jay Robinow glances back from his custom-made three-wheeler. The Des Moines native said of his trike: "There are absolutely no advantages to riding it. I ride it strictly for grins." It actually was heavier than a commercial bike and a bit harder to pedal.
Photo by Harry Baumert

▼ Hey! That's not a bike, 1978. *Photo by Larry E. Neibergall*

▼▼ RAGBRAI has a very diverse and unusual group of bikes including this bicycle built for three. *Photo by Gary Fandel*

Safety a heady concern

By John Karras
(Register Staff Writer)

Bicycle safety begins with . . .

Brushing your teeth in the morning? Nooooo. Eating a hearty breakfast? Nooooo.

Looking both ways before crossing the street? Nooooo.

Bicycle safety begins with your head because that's what you put inside your helmet every time you go for a ride, and because your brains are the one thing you really don't want scrambled if you're in a bicycling accident.

You don't have to run into a wall or get hit by a car to suffer serious damage to your bare head.

Try this: Drop a cantaloupe four feet onto pavement and watch the result. Your head is a little harder, but not much, and the contents are a lot more valuable.

As you probably already guessed, all of this has something to do with the Register's Annual Great Bicycle Ride Across Iowa-XX, July 19-25, of which Chuck (Iowa Boy) Offenburger and I are co-hosts.

If we could require helmets, we would. Such a requirement would be impossible to enforce, so we beg, plead, implore, entreat (I'm into Roget now), beseech, adjure, pester, plague, wheedle, cajole and coax you into wearing one.

We've been making a big deal out of safety consciousness on RAGBRAI for years, but this year -- the first year of RAGBRAI management by trail boss Jim Green, in for Don Benson -- we're making an even bigger deal of it.

I equate riding safely with riding sensibly. Isn't it sensible to do what you can to preserve life and limb?

We have a safety committee this year, the Ride Right Committee. Tim Lane of Des Moines, a veteran RAGBRAI rider, is chairman. Members are from throughout the state, and auxiliary committees and groups have been organized in all of this year's host communities.

Many safety activities, exhibits and awards are planned during the course of RAGBRAI week.

For example, there will be a wheelchair obstacle course at the first couple of host communities, the message being that if you think a helmet is a nuisance, try this.

The Des Moines Register: June 21, 1992

▲ **Helmet décor**, 1982.
Photo by Rick Rickman

◀ **Washington County Sheriff** Yale Jarvis sports what he calls a Brookville SWAT team helmet, complete with working lights and siren, while riding tandem with RAGBRAI pa Jim Hanshaw, (left), 1997
Photo by Warren Taylor

▸ **Amy Brown** of Brookfield, Wisconsin, wears the Team Ben D. Bunny mascot, 1999. *Photo by Doug Wells*

Dan Davidchik of Illinois with ⟨hi⟩s viking helmet. His ride name is ⟨"H⟩elsinki Bob," 1995.
⟨Ph⟩oto by Rodney White

Bryon Nelson, 39, of Moline, Il-⟨li⟩nois, shows off his helmet telling ⟨e⟩veryone he's a member of Team ⟨B⟩one. He says the rawhide bone ⟨is⟩ "quite heavy," and he does ⟨n⟩eck exercises before he rides. ⟨H⟩e reports he's popular with the ⟨d⟩ogs along the route, 1999. *Photo ⟨by⟩ Harry Baumert*

Rider makes a pig of himself.

▲ **Iowa Prairie Network** board member Pam White of Oskaloosa shows off her prairie flowers. They are Ironweed, Blazing Star and Rattlesnake Master, 2001. *Photo by Warren Taylor*

▼ **Roger Fortener** of Waterville, Ohio, tells the story that on his first bike trip 20 years ago, all he had to eat was Spam, so now the Spam goes where he goes, which was a rest stop in Underwood, 1997. *Photo by Amanda Saslow*

▲ **Chris Rapp** of Bozeman, Montana, sports a headgear of toilet paper, sometimes necessity on the ride, 2001. *Photo by Doug Wells*

◄ **Stylish helmets** are a must for the fashion-savvy RAGBRAI rider. This one was spotted in Bussey during RAGBRAI XXVIII, 2000.
Photo by Mary Chind

▼ **Leah Tolsin** and her daisy helmet, 1995.
Photo by Rodney White

▲ **Bill Mondt** of San Diego, California, is none the cooler wearing a propeller that spins in the wind. He is a Boone native, 1999.
Photo by Bob Modersohn

◄ **Les Stellish** of Cherokee has an ear of corn on his helmet. He's a member of the "Popcorn Peddlers," 1999. *Photo by Harry Baumert*

◄ **Bennett O'Connor** of Fort Dodge, a member of team Tutu, takes a turn through Ashton, 1999. *Photo by Gary Fandel*

▼ **Helmets are important** for everyone. This boney rider straps on his helmet and heads down the highway with a good friend on RAGBRAI XV, 1987.
Photos by Bill Nelbergall

▸ **Even four-legged** creatures can enjoy RAGBRAI when they have the right equipment. Kathy Schubert, a rider from Chicago, Illinois, brought her 6-year-old miniature schnauzer Joey along for the ride. Joey even has his own helmet, 1999.
Photo by Gary Fandel

▾ **Joey** gets to ride in style complete with his own umbrella to shield him from the weather, 1999.
Photo by Gary Fandel

Ryan Mable, 3, of Des Moines sucks his thumb while he waits for his dad, Dave Mable, who is a few feet away getting water ...om a sprinkler that was hooked up for RAGBRAI riders to use as they go down Main Street in Roland, 1998. Many youngsters ...e towed along in the ride each year. *Photo by Tina Yee*

▲ **Team Cobra member** Terry Nessa of Webster City unloads a bike from his team's pile in Adel. Nessa said the team piles the bikes so they can remember where they are (usually the first bar on the right when they come into a town), 2000. *Photo by Gary Fandel*

▶ **Bike fitted** with special handlebars, 1991.
Photo by Bill Neibergall

▲ **Two thumbs up** from these participants in RAGBRAI XXII. *Photo by Harry Baumert*

◄ **Steve VanDeest,** who can't use his legs, uses arm power to crank his way on RAGBRAI XXIII, while his sister, Carla VanDeest, pedals from behind. The front wheel of her bike has been removed and the fork attached behind Steve's seat. They are from Waterloo. *Photo by Harry Baumert*

▲ **A RAGBRAI rider** on a recumbent bike waves as he passes a farm while leaving Madrid on day 5 of RAGBRAI XXIX.
Photo by Mary Chind

▶ **Rider with** aerodynamic recumbent bike makes his way between Council Bluffs and Red Oak during RAGBRAI XIV, 1986. *Photo by Loup Langton*

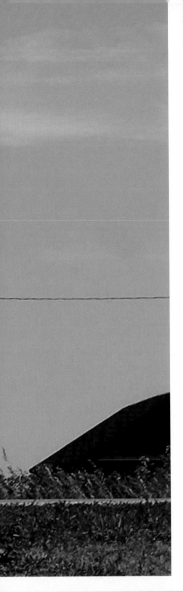

◂ **Disabled biker** David Burds bikes around his apartment complex in Rockville, Maryland, with his custom made bike in preparation for RAGBRAI XXV.
Photo by Ryan Gardner

▾ **Charlie Townsend** of St. Paul, Minnesota, and his children Susie, 9 and Jimmy, 7, ride on a bike built for four. The youngest member of the team, four-year-old Beth, was spending the day with grandparents, 1999.
Photo by Harry Baumert

▶ **A rider cruises** on a recumbent bike with aerodynamic covering on the way to Wadena during RAGBRAI XXVII.
Photo by Bob Modersohn

▼ **These riders** greet the sun south of Harlan as they pedal their tandem recumbent bike on their way to Greenfield, 2000.
Photo by Doug Wells

John Kaplan, St. Paul, Minnesota, heads toward Council Bluffs and the start of RAGBRAI XXVIII on his recumbent three-wheeler loaded up with all his gear. He put in about 400 miles before the start of the official ride. *Photo by Gary Fandel*

Camping

J UST SOME THINGS I'VE NOTICED while roaming around RAGBRAI campgrounds morning and night looking for pictures…

It's hard to find friends. You might run into them by accident, or end up standing next to them in the shower line, but it's easy to get lost. Message boards help, but felt tip markers run and smudge up in the rain. Lots of tents look alike, especially at night after partying on the town square. Of course settling down to sleep in the wrong tent can be a great way to make new friends.

There are unwritten rules that should be posted on RAGBRAI campgrounds. Here are a few:

The sound that a slamming KYBO door makes gets louder as the night gets longer.

Tent ropes are almost invisible at night.

No matter where you shower there is never any privacy, or hot water.

It can rain inside a tent.

If you come across a KYBO with no line in front of it, use it if you need to or not.

The teams that bring along their own chefs eat better than those that don't.

Some people don't sleep in tents, or sleeping bags, and don't seem to have changes of clothing.

Never turn down offers of food.

If not staked down, tents will blow away.

The interesting thing about photographing RAGBRAI is that camping gives you a perspective that shows in your pictures. There's a popular bumper sticker you see around RAGBRAI each year that reads "Bike it, love it." Once you've camped on RAGBRAI you've lived it.

— Doug Wells, photographer
The Des Moines Register

▲ **Herschel Edwards** of Marshalltown sleeps in Ida Grove park after the first day of the ride, 1977. *Photo by Jim Selzer*

◀ **A RAGBRAI rider** rests and reads the newspaper with the headline "Nixon: I Withheld Evidence," 1974. *Photo by David Le*

▼ **Wanda Sturgeon** of Woodward relaxes with a soft drink and newspaper after setting up camp at the fairground in Onawa, 1977. *Photo by David Peterson*

▲ **Fred Schwink,** 15, of Indianola rests after setting up camp at a park in Onawa, 1977.
Photo by David Lewis

◄ **Kicking back in Sigourney** during RAGBRAI III, 1975. *Photo by Warren Taylor*

▸ **Enjoying a quick breakfast** before setting out from Charles City, 1982. *Photo by Harry Baumert*

▾ **Camping gear** for SAGBRAI (Second Annual Great Bicycle Ride Across Iowa), 1974.
Photo by Warren Taylor

▲ **Once bicyclists arrived** in Perry, there was difficulty finding friends and other information. This was made easier by a bulletin board in the city park that carried such messages, 1980.
Photo by George Ceolla

◄ **Burt Payne III** rests in his hammock strung between two posts on a shelter house, 1980. Payne was the third rider to arrive in Atlantic. It was his third RAGBRAI, but the first that he had biked to from his home in Boston, a distance of 1308 miles that he made in 11 days.

▲ **Steve Whitels,** 14, of Forest City, rides through tent city at Ida Grove, 1977. *Photo by David Lewis*

◄ **Vern Bakeman,** 77, entertains RAGBRAI riders from the back of a pickup truck in Rockford, 1982. *Photo by Harry Baumert*

▲ **Team Mystery Machine** of Des Moines unloads gear in Council Bluffs, RAGBRAI XX-VIII. *Photo by Gary Fandel*

◄ **Colin Lamb** of Des Moines hands down bikes to fellow Team Mystery Machine members in the Council Bluffs campground. The team is one of many joining forces for RAGBRAI XXVIII. *Photo by Gary Fandel*

▼ **A RAGBRAI rider** makes a pre-trip adjustment in Missouri Valley, 1997. *Photo by Amanda Saslow*

Bike parking was not easy to find in Montezuma as the bikers rode in for breakfast, 2001. Christa Watson and Leah Lammer of Iowa City squeeze their bikes into the bike rack as they stop at the second stop, Montezuma, along the RAGBRAI ride from Grinnell to Coralville.

Photo by Andrea Melendez

▸ Licensed massage therapist Chris Sparks of Cedar Rapids works on a sore RAGBRAI rider at the Iowa Sports Massage Team tent in Charles City, 1996. A number of therapists set up shop at the RAGBRAI overnight towns, soothing the aching muscles of many.
Photo by Harry Baumert

▾ Brady Becker of Rockwell was selling Christmas tree ornaments as souvenirs in Dougherty, 1999.
Photo by Gary Fandel

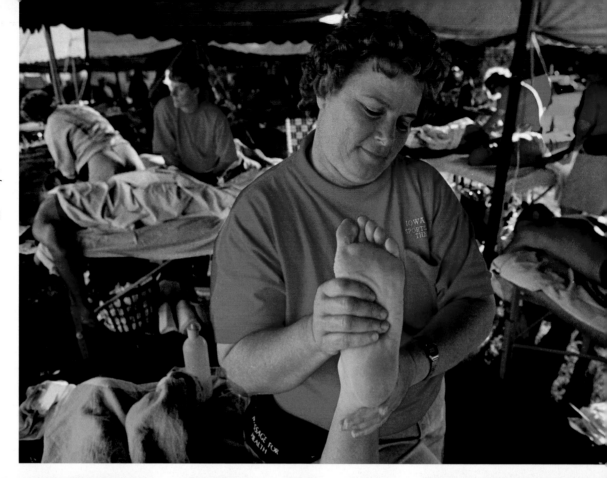

◄ **Riders add** their signatures to a brick wall, commemorating RAGBRAI's pass through Searsboro, 2001.
Photo by Harry Baumert

▼ **Camping** by a pond in Ida Grove, 1988.
Photo by Doug Wells

In St. Ansgar, bikers took a break from riding to dance to music, 1996.
Photo by Crista Jeremiason

The day before RAGBRAI XXVII, riders move into Rock Rapids. One rider makes a pit stop before the crowds hit.
Photo by Gary Fandel

A cyclist passes the campground in Ottumwa where RAGBRAI participants settle for the evening, 2001. *Photo by Harry Baumert*

▸ **One of the tents** set up at University of Northern Iowa in Cedar Falls, 1998, was decorated with various animals and flowers. The animals made their species sound if you walked in front of them. The tent was decorated by a member of Team Loon of Minnesota. *Photo by Tina Yee*

▾ **Jerry Woodhead** of Iowa City BIC Club works on his bicycle in Council Bluffs. RAGBRAI XXVIII was Woodhead's 11th trip across the state as part of the ride. *Photo by Gary Fandel*

▲ **Brian Witt,** left, Gail Witt and Denny Kenealy put together a tent in preparation for a pancake breakfast for RAGBRAI riders in Beebeetown, 1997. The breakfast was sponsored by the Beebeetown little league.
Photo by Sher Stoneman

◀ **Julia Berenguel,** 14, of Des Moines plays a word search game outside her tent at her campground on 11th Avenue in Eldora, 1998.   *Photo by Tina Yee*

▼ **RAGBRAI XXVIII riders** Su Allen, left, of Denver, Colorado, and Beck Eskov of Harlan put up their tent in Council Bluffs. Both are on Team Huff 'n' Puffers of Harlan. Allen was one of the original founders of the team.
Photo by Gary Fandel

◀ **Cool accommo-
dations** in Cedar
Falls, 1989. The
University of North-
ern Iowa commis-
sioned Jim White,
senior professor of
sculpture at Arizona
State University at
Tucson, to create
a unique campsite
experience. The 144
tentlike structures
were turned into a
neon-light sculp-
ture at night.
Photo by Terry Farris

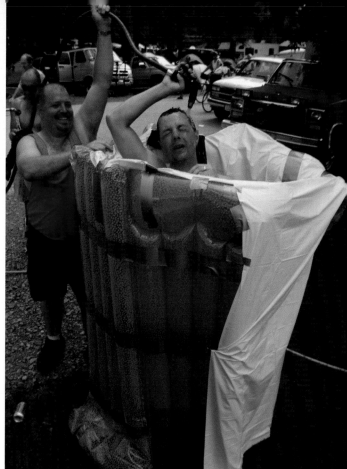

▲ **John McCarthy** helps Team Sticks and Bushes team-mate Mark Wagner use the team's private shower at the Ottumwa campground, 2000. They assembled the device with air mattresses and duct tape. *Photo by Harry Baumert*

◄ **Teammates** Kay Capps of Colorado Springs, Colorado, and Shala Burtsfield of Liberal, Kansas, share a shower in Spencer, 1999. *Photo by Gary Fandel*

◄ ▼ **Dan Oldehoeft,** 29, of Manhattan, Kansas, takes advantage of the free water at a Cass County Fairgrounds livestock building to take a shower, 2001. *Photo by Tina Yee*

▼ **Tim Stapel** and Bolette Albertsen, both of California, cool off with water flowing from a pipe in Keosauqua, 1997. *Photo by Amanda Saslow*

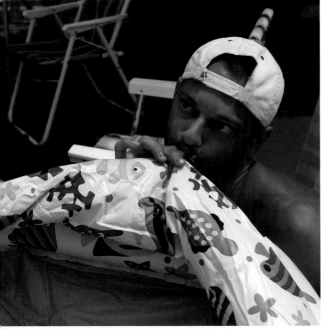

▲ **Resplendent** in pink boa, Diana Cooper of Rocton, Illinois, has way too much fun squirting onlookers in downtown Guthrie Center, 2001. *Photo by Warren Taylor*

◄▲ **Sandy Brooks** of Denver, Colorado, takes advantage of a blanket left out for riders to use at a farmhouse near Maxwell, 2001. *Photo by Mary Chind*

◄ **Brian White** of Des Moines blows up a wading pool to be used as a spa for tired feet at the campground in Perry, 2001. *Photo by Mary Chind*

◄ **Blake Anderson**, 14, of Mason City and Jennifer Valin, 24, of Des Moines ride teeter-totters in Milton. Anderson, on his first RAGBRAI, said the play equipment's wide seat was a welcome change from his bicycle's narrow saddle, 1997. *Photo by Harry Baumert*

▲ **Members of Huff 'N' Puffers** team out of Harlan change roles in the Land of Irwin. From left, Jay Wesselink of River Forest, Illinois, Shirley Troll of Harlan, Mike McNabb of Houston, Texas, and Dave Nadolski of Hackensack, New Jersey, 2001. *Photo by Doug Wells*

▸ **Chrispi Pestalozzi** repairs a bicycle in Arthur, 2001. Pestalozzi works for Harper's Bicycling & Fitness in Muscatine. Mechanics find plenty of business on RAGBRAI. *Photo by Gary Fandel*

▾ **Darton Simons** of Kansas City, Misssouri, picks his way through the heap of luggage in search of his father's duffel bag at Blank Park Zoo, Des Moines, 1997. *Photo by Amanda Saslow*

▲ **Bicycles,** as many veteran RAGBRAI riders can tell you, easily double as a clothesline in a pinch, 1999.
Photo by Doug Wells

◄ **Sue O'Dell** of Littleton, Colorado, gets a gentle nibble from Paulie, a longhorn calf in Parnell, 2001.
Photo by Harry Baumert

▶ **A campground marker** and a bike wheel with missing spokes are left behind in McHose Park in Boone after the riders headed off towards Eldora, 1998. *Photo by Bob Nandell*

▼ **Troy Green** and Dina Nightingale, both of Des Moines and both first-time RAGBRAI riders, relax after reaching a Decorah campground near the Luther campus, 2001. Green rode 100 miles Thursday; Nightingale did the same the day before. *Photo by Bob Modersohn*

Hometown

RAGBRAI riders descend upon Beebeetown, 1991. Photo by Doug Wells

WHEN RAGBRAI ROLLS THROUGH Iowa each year, towns along the way enthusiastically welcome their visitors, treating them as honorary citizens-for-a-day.

At times, hosts literally roll out the carpet. You'll sometimes see rugs spread on railroad tracks over which cyclists must pass, covering the rails to help prevent spills.

The message is clear: "Welcome to our hometown."

Main streets resemble county fair midways, especially at lunch and overnight stops. Teeming crowds of hungry, tired riders flow among food stands, entertainment offerings and shady parks. Local residents have planned for months and are bound to show their burg's best side. After all, in a few hours the guests will be gone. Better make the most of the opportunity.

Pride, a sense of humor and genuine friendliness combine to make memories for riders. One town constructed a welded arch of bicycle frames under which bicyclists rode. Another set aside several old frames on a side street for a "bicycle toss" contest. Creative folks have arranged hay bales into a bicycle sculpture and painted a bundle of hundreds of plastic milk jugs to resemble a giant ear of corn.

Hospitality isn't just things set up for visitors' amusement. It's the delight of children standing along the road, offering high fives to passing cyclists, then getting sprayed by streams from water bottles. It's the unabashed curiosity of a resident, questioning a newcomer about some gizmo on her two-wheeler.

Local talent - dancers, singers, musicians - love to perform and invite visitors to join in.

Ask riders why they come from across the U.S. and around the world to join this traveling party and you'll hear many reasons. But high on the list will be the sense of community displayed to them countless times each day of the ride.

— Harry Baumert, photographer
The Des Moines Register

▲ **Allen Thenkle** and daughter Laura take a break at the library in Battle Creek, 1977. *Photo by Jim Selzer*

◀ **Donald Kaul** and John Karras, co-hosts of RAGBRAI, are presented the key to the city in Fort Madison by Mayor E. R. Rainey, 1975.
Photo by Frank Folwell

▶ **Water** on the ride from Perry to Eldora, 1986. *Photo by Warren Taylor*

A banner in Fort Madison welcomes bike riders to the city, 1975. *Photo by Frank Folwell*

◄Longtime Polk City banker Bill Miller, 69, talks with Rhonda Bombei, 25, of Coralville, in Polk City, 1983. *Photo by Warren Taylor*

▸Raquel Miller, left, and Henry Ka Lampert of Ames hoist a beer while cooling off in a local pub's trough at Steamboat Rock during RAGBRAI XI. In the background is Jay Smith of Sioux City. *Photo by Warren Taylor*

▾Talking with the locals, 1978. *Photo by Larry E. Neibergall*

▲ **RAGBRAI riders** were rocking out in Danbury, much to the delight of, from left, Margaret Twitchell and Bernice Gahan of Danbury and their friend Arleen Kellen of Omaha, Nebraska. They just thought it was great. Dancing is Sandy Wood of the Blue Hen team of Wilmington, Delaware, 1995. *Photo by Doug Wells*

◄ **Making good** on their boast that Washington is the cleanest city in Iowa, the residents opened their shower doors to RAGBRAI riders over-nighting there. Ethel Cavin, left, hands a towel to Chicago-area rider Julie Miller after Miller showered in Calvin's basement, 1986. *Photo by Warren Taylor*

▼ **Cooling down** the riders near Hudson, 1978. *Photo by David Lewis*

◄◄ **RAGBRAI XVI Riders** follow the route through the streets of downtown Des Moines, 1988. *Photo by Robert Nandell*

◄ **Riders flood downtown** Joice during RAGBRAI XV, 1987. *Photo by Doug Wells*

▼ **Riders jam the streets** of Clarinda during RAGBRAI XVII, 1989. *Photo by Doug Wells*

▲ **Arch welcomes riders** to Clarinda, 1989. *Photo by Doug Wells*

▶ **Riders** come into downtown Des Moines, 1992. *Photo by Gary Miller*

▼ **Sign welcomes riders** to Killduff during the 1991 ride.
Photo by Warren Taylor

Population explosion in small town of Sibley

By JOHN KARRAS
(Register Staff Writer)

Sibley, Ia. - I've seen this ing on 24 years now, but it still astonishing to me how small wa communities can stretch emselves out to accommodate event as large and as demand-g as RAGBRAI.

Sibley's population is about 000. RAGBRAI XXIV's popu-ion probably is around 12,000, unting the drivers of support hicles and other family mem-rs along for the fun of it.

Yet Sibley, like dozens of Iowa wns before it, appeared to have erything under control as the rde arrived from Sioux Center nday.

Lila Hattig, Sibley's AGBRAI co-chairwoman with elley Morris, said there was a oment of panic at 6 a.m. Sunday en the committee realized that re were no portable toilets at e main campground around the hool grounds.

"But then someone mentioned at those were being supplied The Register and just hadn't ived yet," she said.

There were other problems, of course - there always are - but the town's RAGBRAI committee appeared to have handled them all with dispatch.

Lois DeBerg, for example, said her housing committee had placed at least 350 groups with private homes, either staying inside or camping in yards, "and there had to be at least another 100 that contacted families privately," she said.

Pretty good for a town of 3,000.

As you might expect, Sibley was using just about every available square foot of space for RAGBRAI camping.

In addition to the capacious school grounds, tents were springing up in three city parks and at the county fairgrounds.

Sunday also was the last day of the county fair. The fair board had sent the exhibitors home a day early (they usually stay through Sunday) to make room for the RAGBRAI campers, but kept the midway, food stands and evening entertainment going for the bikers.

The Sibley fun began right at the entrance to town, where bleachers were set up for townspeople applauding and cheering the bikers as they rode through an arch built for the day.

The fun continued through the afternoon and evening with performances by the Seattle Cascades, a precision drum and bugle corps from Seattle, Wash.; the Cruisers, a local classic rock group; Pojamas, a four-piece eclectic rock and country band from Galena, Ill.; Terry Bloes and Marti Vast-Binder, a clown team that has been inducted into the Midwest Clown Hall of Fame; and an impromptu talent show.

Lila Hattig was asked about other problems and responded with tales of an imminent Sibley population explosion.

Apparently three women intimately associated with the RAGBRAI effort either gave or are about to give birth.

Dale Honken's wife had a girl last Saturday. Honken, head of the information booth committee, had told his workers they could park in his driveway near the booth on RAGBRAI day, but only if his wife, Karen, had already had the baby.

Amy Van Marel, hospitality chairwoman, was at the welcoming arch Sunday morning at 6:30, schlepping boxes of T-shirts and painting signs. Her baby is due any moment.

And Kyle Grimes, beverage garden chairman, may have to get his wife, Marilee, to the hospital at any moment for the delivery of twins.

Is Sibley growing or what?

Assisting Hattig and Morris, in addition to the committee heads noted above, were:

Lois Fleming and Jean Kennedy, volunteer recruitment; Chris Godfredsen, publicity; Roxanne Heinrichs and Jolene Eddy, campgrounds; Randy Francis and Harold Dawson, entertainment; Suzette Grady and Julie Mohr, food vendors; Jody Nasers, housing; Renee Reinholdt, hospitality; Mitchell Watter, public safety; Gary Obbink, electrical; Tom Snyder, Ride Right; Chad Vogel, beverage garden; Paul Adkins, law enforcement; and Jay Mohr, advisory board.

Today we descend on Estherville.

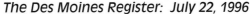

The Des Moines Register: July 22, 1996

Matt Heerema, 15, Webster City plays e trumpet and elcomes riders to s community, 1995. ay bales resembling castle were stacked the entrance to e town. *Photo by Jeffrey Carney*

▲ **Rolly Hart** of Indianola greets riders as they make their way under an arch of balloons at the entrance to the Indianola town square, 1997. *Photo by Amanda Saslow*

▶ **Christina Clevenger,** 12, holding sign, and Marie Corrin, 12, direct riders to the pancake breakfast in Beebeetown, 1997. *Photo by Sher Stoneman*

▼ **RAGBRAI riders** swarm in the town of Paullina, 1996. *Photo by Kevin Wolf*

▼▶ **Bikers ride** over carpet-covered railroad tracks as they enter Carpenter, 1996. Townspeople provided the covering to prevent spills. *Photo by Harry Baumert*

Team Ducks takes a breakfast break in Ocheydan. From left are Dan Pleis, Jon avis, Cindy Uttal, Eric Swanstrom and Brendan Zimmermann, 1996.
oto by Crista Jeremiason

Bob Beekman of Pocahontas adds ice to his ice cream maker at a stand east Lebanon, 1997. *Photo by Harry Baumert*

Recorded music plays from the bandstand in downtown Milo as Conny Sheil Indianola dances with her golden retriever, Mikki, 1997. *Photo by Harry Baumert*

Mike Bricker of Kahoka, Missouri, finishes a drink outside The Village Creamery Keosauqua before resuming the trek to Fairfield, 1997. *Photo by Harry Baumert*

▸ **A bicycle** festooned with lights is parked near a sign reading "Ft. Madison 464 miles" at the campground, 1997.
Photo by Amanda Saslow

▾ **Beams of** laser light flash through the darkness as thousands of bicycle riders take in the show at the Blank Park Zoo, 1997.
Photo by Bill Neibergall

▲ **Bicycles and bicyclists** swarm the streets of Dike, 1998, as RAGBRAI XXVI sweeps through town. *Photo by Sher Stoneman*

◄ **RAGBRAI riders** roll into Craig on a hot Sunday morning, 1998. More than 10,000 cyclists passed through the town on their way from the ride's starting point, Hawarden, to Cherokee. *Photo by Sher Stoneman*

▼ **Mark Crown** of Omaha, Nebraska, paused on Galva's Main Street to enjoy a cooling spray of water and a chat with RAGBRAI spectator DuWayne Vogt, 1998. *Photo by Tina Yee*

Tom Lindblom of Lindblom Services Inc. carries a hefty load of toilet paper in Hawarden, 1998.
Photo by Sher Stoneman

Jeanie and Glen Visser of Harvey dance to live music by The Country Bits and Pieces in Craig, 1998.
Photo by Sher Stoneman

Members of Team Putz dance to "YMCA" in Wellsburg. Members include, from left, Tom Fitch, Marty McHone and Danielle Welch. Joining them is David Bratt, with beard, 1998. *Photo by Tina Yee*

Judy McKenney stamps a passport for Kathy Hemsley of Philadelphia, Pennsylvania. Some riders stop at all the towns along the route to get their RAGBRAI passports stamped, 1998. *Photo by Sher Stoneman*

St. Luke's Catholic Church is a backdrop as Pam Hammes, of Sigourney pedals to the top of the hill e route to Ft. Atkinson, 1999.
Photo by Harry Baumert

Nick Gordon of Kensett and Brandon Diedrich of Grafton try to cool off in the shade of a tree in Remsen, 1998. *Photo by Sher Stoneman*

▲ **Tony Smith**, 11, of Dubuque holds his cousin Scott Kruse, 2, of Carmel, Indiana, as they exchange high-fives with riders west of Zwingle, 1999. *Photo by Harry Baumert*

▶ **Howard Nue** of New York City, New York, prepares to leave West Union after adding to the box full of empty beverage containers, 1999. *Photo by Harry Baumert*

▼ **A giant bicycle** made from balloons greets riders as they make their way into Manchester, 1999. *Photo by Bob Modersohn*

▲ **"The Tubador,"** also known as Gary McCurdy of Washington, gets a smooch during RAGBRAI XXVII in Mallard. The appreciative listener is Cheryl Lindgren of Altoona. *Photo by Gary Fandel*

◄ **In Titonka,** RAGBRAI XXVII bikers had the main street to themselves.
Photo by Doug Wells

▲ **Peter Venuti** of Beverly, Massachusetts, competes in the bike toss at Ossian, 1999. *Photo by Harry Baumert*

▲ **Dewey Wellendorf,** chairman of the Ashton RAGBRAI welcome committee, greets riders with a honk, 1999. *Photo by Gary Fandel*

▲▶ **Rock Rapids** finds its own unique method to greet RAGBRAI XXVII riders – with bicycles attached to poles along Main Street. *Photo by Doug Wells*

◀ **Norbert Hackman,** Gene Boyer, Robert Meyer and Loras Reicks pass the time in St. Lucas by watching riders enter the town, 1999.
Photo by Harry Baumert

▼ **Jan Tiernan** of Minneapolis, Minnesota, gets her picture taken by Jill Jacobs of Chicago, Illinois, in front of the giant ear of corn made from plastic milk jugs on the outskirts of Alpha, 1999. *Photo by Bob Modersohn*

▲ **A mud hole** in Melvin provides cool relief for Lindsay Carlson, bottom, and Denise Haag, both of Bradley, Illinois, 1999. *Photo by Gary Fandel*

▲▸ **Judy Hudson** of Topeka, Kansas, puts out tie-dye T-shirts for RAGBRAI XXVII in Rock Rapids. *Photo by Gary Fandel*

▸ **In Ankeny,** Niccie Kliegl of Orange City has her photo taken with Santa Claus, a.k.a. Southeast Elementary Principal Denny Warren, 2000. *Photo by Mary Chind*

▾ **Paige Schreiner,** 6, extends greetings to RAGBRAI XXVIII riders as they enter Ottumwa. *Photo by Harry Baumert*

▾▾ **Gina Interrante** of the Decorah Cycle Club limbos to the music at a restaurant in Harlan, 2000. *Photo by Gary Fandel*

In Shelby, Larry Blecha of the Jolly Home Brewers, has fun entertaining the crowd, 2000. *Photo by Doug Wells*

▸ **Chester Schmidt** welcomes riders into Exira. Schmidt is the mascot for the Exira Vikings, 2000.
Photo by Gary Fandel

▾ **A day to dance:** Betsy McCormick, center, of Boyne Falls, Michigan, dances with Team Whiner in Minden, 2000.
Photo by Doug Wells

▲ **Lindsey Garwood,** 8, left, and her sister Kaylee, 4, swing in front of their home as riders go through Dexter on RAGBRAI XXVIII. *Photo by Michael Kaire*

◄ **Bright welcome:** Cyclists arrive in Shelby through an arch of colorful bicycles, 2000. *Photo by Gary Fandel*

▼◄ **RAGBRAI XXVIII riders breeze past** the Danish windmill in Elk Horn, 2000. *Photo by Doug Wells*

▼► **CAM cheerleaders** Carrie Euken, Melinda Brahms and Jennifer Miller perform for riders in Anita to raise money for their squad to buy new uniforms, 2000. *Photo by Doug Wells*

▶ **RAGBRAI XXVIII**
participants flow into
Adel on their way to
Ankeny. Many took
a break here on the
Dallas County Court-
house lawn, 2000.
Photo by Gary Fandel

▸**Outside of Greenfield** the town's RAGBRAI XXVIII welcoming committee greeted riders from under the wings of a plane. *Photo by Doug Wells*

▸▾**Melissa Cook,** left, of Lincoln, Missouri, and Trish Chandler of Branson, Missouri, ride a hay bike in Neola. Marlin Hammond, also of Lincoln, captures the sight on film, 2000. *Photo by Gary Fandel*

▾**Deep River's** unofficial farewell committee waves to riders leaving their town, 2001. From left they are Fern Taylor, Phyllis Smith, Dottie Schwertfeger and Delores Schmidt. *Photo by Warren Taylor*

▾▾ **Riders queue up** for breakfast at the community center in Bouton, 2001. *Photo by Robert Nandell*

Nuns on the Run of Danbury bless Kim Jahn of Manning in Ida Grove City Park. The faux nuns are, from left, Lorna Uehle, Sharyl Bruning, rlene Cameron, Betty Lansink and Tottie Seuntjens, 2001. *Photo by Doug Wells*

Alex Donan, 11, of Denver, Colorado, provides the bagpipe music for wins Kathleen Maguire, left, of Chicago and Maggie MacGregor of St. Paul, Minnesota, 2001. *Photo by Gary Fandel*

▲ **Riders through Maxwell** make room for Red Reese of Des Moines, who was directing bicyclists to a friend's store, 2001. *Photo by Warren Taylor*

◄ **Bonnie Berquam** of St. Paul, Minnesota, performs her belly dance in Washta, 2001.
Photo by Rodney White

▶ **When you're** only three, a tricycle is likely the preferred mode of transportation. Traves Rice makes his own Great Tricycle Ride Across Morning Sun, 1979.
Photo by Bob Modersohn

▼ **Riders fill the main street** through Manilla on the third day of RAGBRAI XXIX.
Photo by Gary Fandel

▲ **Amy Badger** of Albuquerque, New Mexico, sends e-mail from a Gateway booth in Sioux City. It was her first RAGBRAI and her first time in Iowa, 2001.   *Photo by Rodney White*

The Food

Martha Norman, 75, of Zearing, shows off a butterscotch meringue pie like the one judged "Best of RAGBRAI," 1998. *Photo by Marc Hall*

MOST PEOPLE WOULD THINK an entire week of riding a bicycle across Iowa in the heat (it's the humidity that really counts) of July would result in the loss of few pounds. The truth is, most riders will admit to actually gaining a few pounds. If you have never experienced RAGBRAI, you might find this hard to believe, but it doesn't take long to see the big picture. Locals from almost every town and along the route supply a plethora of food and drink, and that's before you ever get to the host town. You've got churches, chambers, fire departments, little league, scouts, schools, etc. offering pasta, pie, burgers, brats, chops, sweet corn, etc., and of course there's breakfast. Des Moines native and veteran RAGBRAIer Carl Voss has the right idea, he always brakes for pie.

RAGBRAI is an adventure with a range of emotions that can vary from hill to hill. Food is a natural buffer to the stressed rider. Add to that the feeling that you've just taken part in a three-to-four hour aerobics class, pedaling from town to town in the heat and few think to count the calories of the corndog and pie in each hand while taking a break along the route.

RAGBRAI is a cornucopia of tastes and strategies for their preparation. The bratwurst in the pot boiling in Atlantic is different than the one on the grill in Ankeny, which is nothing like the one on the big Amana bun in Coralville. The sweet corn is ripe as the summer starts to mature, and the lemonade is icy cold in a frosted glass at the corner diner. And just when you think you've seen every different food stand and refreshment tent possible, up over a rise near Millerton pops up an Amish cart selling fresh baked goods to hungry morning riders.

— Gary Fandel, photographer
The Des Moines Register

▲ **Watermelon** for everyone, RAGBRAI IV, Muscatine.
Photo by Frank Folwell

◄ **Della Wood,** left, a participant in RAGBRAI III, pitches in to help Louise Shreve, owner of Shreve Café in Luther, after hungry bicyclists swamped the café. Della prepared ham and eggs while other bicyclists helped by serving coffee to the riders. Photo by Warren Taylor

▲ **Enjoying watermelon** during RAGBRAI, 1976. *Photo by David Lewis*

Young entreprenuers set up shop in Grundy Center, 1983. *Photo by Warren Taylor*

▸ **Serious grilling.** Fire up several grills with mouthwatering Iowa meat on a hot summer day and you have a hometown RAGBRAI greeting, 1985. *Photo by Gary Fandel*

Fried chicken in Grundy Center, 1983. *Photo by Warren Taylor*

▲ **Tudy Meyer,** left, JoAnn Ott, Viola Bonfig and Mary Jean Svendsen scramble some 350 dozen eggs at Ossian's Knights of Columbus hall for RAGBRAI XXVII riders. The eggs were donated by Calmar Foods.
Photo by Harry Baumert

▲▶ **Lawrence Dittmer,** right, and Frank Lesch of the Shelby Kiwanis serve up bushels of sweet corn at the park in Shelby, 2000. *Photo by Gary Fandel*

▶ **Kathleen Cook** cuts into a gooseberry pie as JoAnn Turner and Marcia Allen hold umbrellas overhead to keep it dry in Corning, 1997. Turner said the local Presbyterian church "had two pie days," during which members baked 100 pies to feed cyclists.
Photo by Sher Stoneman

Towns along the way never lack in creativity for ways to feed and ntertain their RAGBRAI guests. Local organizers brought out a big top in his community for shade and refreshments.

▶ **Come one, come all:** Ethan Zellmer, 13, of Atlantic advertises treats old by his Cass County 4-H club in Anita, 2000. *Photo by Gary Fandel*

Pork-out in Anamosa, 1994. *Photo by Harry Baumert*

Loy Miller grabs a watermelon in Milo's city park, 1997. He was helping o give away slices of more than 100 melons. *Photo by Harry Baumert*

Battle cry: Pooorrrkk chooppps!

By Kate Kompas
(Register Staff Writer)

Casey, Ia. – Riders see a lot of familiar faces on RAGBRAI.

One in particular makes some otherwise sedate riders scream "Pork chops!" at the top of their lungs.

Thousands of riders every RAGBRAI buy a $6 pork chop from Paul Bernhard, a.k.a. "Mr. Pork Chop."

This is the 17th year for Bernhard, 72, of Bancroft. He sells his specially roasted pork chops served with only a paper towel at a different spot every day along the route.

He has celebrity status with riders. Dozens of them whiz by and yell an exaggerated, "Pooorrrkk chooppps!" in imitation of his famous call.

"I do RAGBRAI for the people," he said. "There's lots of nice people on this ride. Crazy, but nice."

Bernhard said he started doing his "pork chops" battle cry the first year he sold chops on RAGBRAI. That year in Mason City, the rain had broken up the crowds and he had to yell to draw them to his stand.

The novelty has stuck.

The people who weren't buying pork chops from Bernhard were lining up to have their pictures taken with him. Bernhard declines to say how much he sells on RAGBRAI – "I don't ask you what your salary is" – but it's fair to say it's his biggest event of the year.

"I've done jubilees and weddings, but I don't yell like that there. Not in church anyway," Bernhard said.

Bernhard, a past president of Iowa Pork Producers, travels around RAGBRAI in a "sag wagon" of his own. It's painted pink and has "Mr. Pork Chop" written on it.

How many more RAGBRAIs will he do? Bernhard answers: "How much longer am I going to live?"

Daren Osborn, 21, of Ames said he's visited Mr. Pork Chop twice this week. "They're really good. I guess it's the way they cook 'em."

The Des Moines Register: July 26, 2001

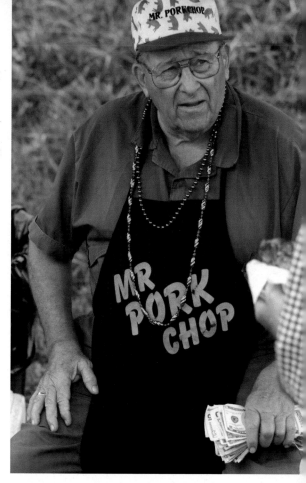

▲ **Paul Bernhard,** a.k.a. Mr. Pork Chop, sells pork chops to RAGBRAI riders along state highway 25, 2001. *Photo by Alex Dorgan-Ross*

▲ **Mary Mueller,** left, and Jo Koob, both of Sioux City, share a piece of pie in the rain at Schaller during day two of RAGBRAI XXIX. *Photo by Doug Wells*

◄ **She's into it:** Marcy Hahn of Sioux City sports bicycle-themed glasses while enjoying a sandwich in Casey, 2001. *Photo by Carl Voss*

▶ **Robyn Plagman,** 19, of Shelby feasts on a cup full of sweet corn served in Shelby by the Shelby Kiwanis, 2000. *Photo by Gary Fandel*

▲ **Riders line up** to buy fruit, hand-cranked ice cream and homemade peanut brittle from an Amish farmer north of Millerton, 1997.
Photo by Harry Baumert

▸ **Rock Rechkemmer,** left, of Maynard and Ken Bafer of Sumner cook pork ribs in Wadena, 1999.
Photo by Bob Modersohn

◂ **Betty Best** helps cut up more than ten dozen pies made by members of St. Luke's Parish in St. Lucas to feed RAGBRAI riders, 1999.
Photo by Harry Baumert

▸ **Pretty corny:** Members of the Monroe United Methodist Church shuck corn in Reasnor. From left is Judy Woody, Scott Van Veen, Rita Van Veen and Jan Phifer, 2000.
Photo by Mary Chind

▾ **Gene Enger** of Emmetsburg chows down on an ear of sweet corn at Ventura, 1999. *Photo by Gary Fandel*

Love & Marriage

Jodie and Stephen Rooks of Orlando, Florida, on their first RAGBRAI, decided to renew their marriage vows at a wedding chapel in Dallas Center, 2000. *Photo by Doug Wells*

LYCRA REPLACES LACE. Gatorade takes the place of champagne. Those who wed on RAGBRAI say it's a fun and spontaneous way to tie the knot without the stress of mailing invitations and sweating the details. While few couples actually marry on the road, many relationships have developed and blossomed there. Where else can you spend a whole week with someone you just met without feeling like you're even dating?

Many couples extend their "togetherness" on RAGBRAI by riding tandem. Jim Neagle explained the RAGBRAI love bug this way, "Relationships are a lot like riding a tandem. You have to communicate, you have to have common goals, you have to work together. If you do, everything goes fine. If you don't somebody gets hurt." Neagle wed his wife Bobbi Wilson in Knoxville during the ride in 1992.

RAGBRAI is full of human effort and emotion. The overriding emotion being joy. The joy of another day of peddling into a headwind finished. The joy of newfound friends and old acquaintances revisited. The joy of sharing the daunting task of traversing an entire state in one short week. The joy of the community among the riders and the cities and towns they visit.

Each year brings more romance, more commitments and more nuptials along the way. Like corndogs and helmets, love and marriage have always been a part of RAGBRAI.

— Mary Chind, photographer
The Des Moines Register

▲ **Dia Brown,** 15, and Randy Moore, 17, both of Ames, celebrate the end of the bike ride with a kiss, 1975. *Photo by Warren Taylor*

◀ **Newlyweds** Eric and Vicky Thran of Nashville, Tennessee, cool their feet in Emmetsburg's Five Island Lake. They were married nine months earlier, but delayed their honeymoon to spend it at RAGBRAI, 1985. *Photo by Gary Fandel*

▼◀ **John Karras** gets his fill in Clinton, 1978. *Photo by David Lewis*

▼▶ **Cedar Rapids natives** Tim Neagle, right, and Bobbi Wilson walk down the isle wearing their helmets in a Knoxville park during a wedding ceremony attended by many RAGBRAI XX riders. *Photo by Jeffrey Z. Carney*

Three RAGBRAI couples renewed their vows in a ceremony presided over by Pastor Don Frank at the Cutler-Donahoe Bridge in Winterset, 1997. *Photo by Sher Stoneman*

Dick and Jane Fortier, of Storm Lake, dance to country music during a RAGBRAI stopover in Searsboro, 2001. *Photo by Harry Baumert*

Bicycles and bridges of Madison County stir thoughts of love

By TARA DEERING
Register Staff Writer

Winterset, Ia. - RAGBRAI riders Bradley Workman and Cindy Willard from Florida, stood in their bike shoes and looked into each others eyes as the Rev. Don Frank performed a wedding renewal service Tuesday at one of the romantic covered bridges of Madison County in Winterset.

But unlike the other two couples who renewed their vows Tuesday afternoon under the Cutler-Donahoe Bridge, Workman and Willard are not married.

"Today I actually proposed to her," Workman said. "I thought it would be a special occasion for both of us to remember."

Workman and Willard have been together for six years and the love between them is evident. Two wedding doll trolls are pinned onto the back of their tandem bicycle. And they both enjoy RAGBRAI.

Even though they participated in the ceremony, Workman had not gotten an official answer from Willard. She said she had to think about it.

Allen and Barbara Thomas from Phoenix, Ariz., celebrated their 25th anniversary by renewing their vows Tuesday.

The Thomases, riding RAGBRAI with their two teenage children and Allen's grandfather and brother, said they decided that morning to renew their wedding vows. Their family didn't even know about it.

"We're celebrating tonight because we don't have to sleep on the ground," Barbara Thomas said. "We were lucky enough to get a motel room in Des Moines."

Lloyd and Sandy Scherlin from Pringhar have only been married a month, but they said the beautiful covered-bridge setting prompted them to renew their vows.

"I thought it would be a neat memory to have," Sandy Scherlin said.

The Des Moines Register: July 23, 1997

◄▲ Jodie and Stephen Rooks of Orlando, Florida, a renewal of marriage vows at a wedding chapel in Dallas Center. Rev. Kalen Frista of the United Methodist Church presides over the ceremony, 2000.
Photo by Doug Wells

▲ Scott Annis, left, and Gwen Husted, right, were married in Perry during RAGBRAI XXIX.
Photo by Rodney White

◄ Newlyweds Dave and Kir Diercks of Shell Rock, who married July 4, kiss after arriving at Blank Park Zoo. The couple spent their honeymoon on RAGBRAI, 1997.
Photo by Bill Neibergall